CRICKET in the THICKET
Poems about Bugs

CAROL MURRAY • illustrated by MELISSA SWEET

Christy Ottaviano Books • HENRY HOLT AND COMPANY • NEW YORK

SOURCES

Amateur Entomologists' Society, amentsoc.org

Camp Kid Scoop. *The Hutchinson News*, 2014–15.

Eaton, Eric R., and Kenn Kaufman. *Kaufman Field Guide to Insects of North America*. New York: Houghton Mifflin, 2007.

Encyclopaedia Britannica, britannica.com

Levi, Herbert W., and Lorna R. Levi. *Spiders and Their Kin: A Golden Guide*. New York: St. Martin's Press, 2002.

National Geographic magazine, nationalgeographic.com

Scientific American magazine, scientificamerican.com

Smithsonian magazine, smithsonian.com

University of Minnesota Monarch Lab, monarchlab.org

With thanks to the Dillon Nature Center, Hutchinson, Kansas.

Henry Holt and Company, *Publishers since 1866*
175 Fifth Avenue, New York, New York 10010 • mackids.com

Henry Holt® is a registered trademark of Macmillan Publishing Group, LLC.
Text copyright © 2017 by Carol Murray
Illustrations copyright © 2017 by Melissa Sweet

Library of Congress Cataloging-in-Publication Data
Names: Murray, Carol, author. | Sweet, Melissa, 1956– illustrator.
Title: Cricket in the thicket : poems about bugs / by Carol Murray ; illustrated by Melissa Sweet.
Description: First edition. | New York : Henry Holt and Company, 2017. |
"Christy Ottaviano Books." | Includes bibliographical references.
Identifiers: LCCN 2016034681 | ISBN 9780805098181 (hardback)
Subjects: | BISAC: JUVENILE NONFICTION / Poetry / General. |
JUVENILE NONFICTION / Animals / Insects, Spiders, etc.
Classification: LCC PS3563.U7645 A6 2017 | DDC 811/.54—dc23
LC record available at https://lccn.loc.gov/2016034681

Our books may be purchased in bulk for promotional, educational, or business use.
Please contact your local bookseller or the Macmillan Corporate and Premium Sales Department
at (800) 221-7945 ext. 5442 or by e-mail at MacmillanSpecialMarkets@macmillan.com.

First edition—2017 / Designed by Patrick Collins
The artist used watercolor and mixed media to create the illustrations for this book.
Printed in China by RR Donnelley Asia Printing Solutions Ltd., Dongguan City, Guangdong Province

3   5   7   9   10   8   6   4

For my two grown sons, Dan and Jack,
whose favorites are still Inchworm, Firefly,
and Grasshopper Green
—C. M.

For Nick, Adrian, and Ben
—M. S.

CONTENTS

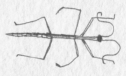

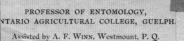

Cricket's Alarm

Cricket in the thicket, *cricket*.

Cricket in the house, *cricket*.

Cricket in the bedroom, not as quiet as a mouse, *cricket*.

Cricket in the closet in a pocket or a shoe, *cricket*.

Cricket,

   Cricket,

      Cricket,

         Cricket.

Where are you?

Only male crickets can chirp. They rub their wings together to create a mating call or to keep other males away. In Japan and China, people keep crickets as pets for their song.

Go, Ants, Go!

Working, while the world is sleeping,
tugging, lugging, running, creeping,
three small letters, that is all.
A-N-T, together, crawl!

There are more ants in the world than any other insect. Some ants live off juices made by other bugs; some eat insects, and some harvest grass, leaves, and berries to eat later. During winter in cold areas, ants sleep in their nests.

8

Cicada's Surprise

She left a treasure on a tree,
    as thin as paper, plain to see.
We showed it to another kid,
    wondering what Cicada did.

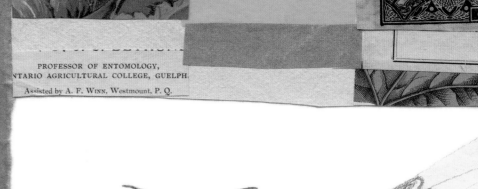

PROFESSOR OF ENTOMOLOGY,
NTARIO AGRICULTURAL COLLEGE, GUELPH.
Assisted by A. F. WINN, Westmount, P. Q.

Cicadas spend from two to seventeen years underground, feeding
on tree roots and emerging as adults. They live in trees and number in
the billions. Cicadas molt, or shed their exoskeletons, on tree trunks.

9

Just Jumping, Spider!

The jumping spider
has a handy-dandy
way to travel.

He spins and winds
a silky thread,
and lets it all unravel.

He keeps his string
inside until
he finds he's moving slow.

Then he'll unlatch
his trusty hatch,
and down the road he'll go.

Jumping spiders are among the most colorful of spiders. Instead of building webs to catch food, they use their silk as a lifeline when they jump in search of dinner. Like most spiders, they have eight eyes, but this type of spider can see especially well.

Dragons Fly the Sky

A lovely wisp,

awash in blue,

with light and lacy wings,

a mini-glider in the sky, who S O A R S

but never stings.

Dragonflies are a human's friend because they helpfully eat mosquitoes and other insects. With four wings, they—like butterflies—are not true flies, which have only two wings.

11

Inchworming Along

Inchworm travels down the trail,
swifter than a slippery snail—
up and down, around and through,
making haste with worm's-eye view.
She has a dream, a special plot.
She's measuring for a garden spot.

Inchworms are similar to caterpillars. They crawl by
alternately stretching their front forward and then bringing
up their rear to meet it. Also called measuring worms or
loopers, inchworms are the larvae of moths.

Ladybug Hug

Everyone loves the ladybug.
She's cute and small and shy,
a bright, delightful, friendly sort
and pleasing to the eye.

A charming little insect,
bringing polka-dotted fun.
So should you want to hug a bug,
this lady is the one.

Surprise! That ladybug may actually be male—it's hard to tell.
Ladybugs are said to bring good luck. A gardener's helper,
ladybugs rid the garden of aphids, which can damage plants.

13

Trees and Knees and Bumblebees

Rumble, rumble,
Bumblebee.
Don't you know
you're bugging me?

Your buzzing
in the climbing tree
may make me tumble,
Bumblebee.

Stop that rumble,
Bumblebee.
Perhaps I'll stumble
as I flee.

I'll crash and crumble,
skin my knee,
and then I'll grumble,
Bumblebee.

 Most bumblebees are black and yellow with fine hair covering their bodies. They have long tongues, like straws, for gathering nectar. Many flowers would be extinct without the help of the bumblebee.

Let's Hear It for Dung Beetle!

I don't get much respect, and I suspect you didn't know
that I was very popular in Egypt long ago.

A sacred bug. Oh yes, indeed! A charm with magic power.
Too bad you didn't know me in my former, finest hour.

Dung beetles are ground dwellers and especially like manure piles.
They live off the waste of animals, particularly plant eaters like
cows and camels. In ancient Egypt, some dung beetles were called
scarabs. Ornaments in the form of scarabs have been found on
mummies.

15

Water Beetles Got Talent

I'm spotted like a puppy dog,
a most unusual thing.

I carry little pods of air
beneath each shiny wing.

I creep and crawl and glide the sky,
I'm begging for your vote.

I've got a lot of talent,
I can flip—and fly—and float!

Spotted water beetles are sleek and streamlined, built for swimming. They are athletes and can breathe underwater with air they carry beneath their wings. A repellent fluid protects them from fish.

Roly-Poly Afternoon

Holy moly! Roly-poly bugs
are everywhere.
They hide beside the slippery slide
and gather here and there.

They like to lodge in camouflage,
all rolled up in a ball,
but a gentle nudge will make them budge,
and then they start to crawl.

And though they're not the kind of friend
you'd like to spend the day with,
in slow and sleepy quiet times,
they sure are fun to play with.

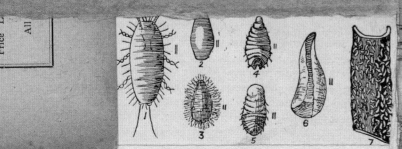

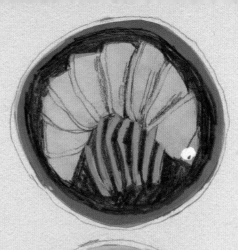

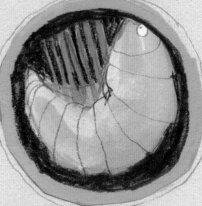

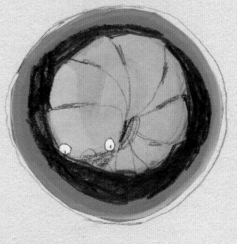

Roly-polies are also called pill bugs. They
are actually crustaceans, like shrimp and
crayfish, and have seven pairs of legs.

17

Walking Stick Courage

If it's skinny
like a twig—
and it looks
like a twig—
and it feels
like a twig—
then—
it must be a twig.

C'mon, let's touch it.
You first!

Walking sticks are usually brown or green
and many have wings. Their strange
sticklike appearance is their camouflage
and protects them from predators.

Praying or Preying?

Pray tell us, Mr. Mantis,
do you prey or simply pray?

Do you scout about for victims
or fold your hands all day?

You look a little scary,
but appearances deceive.

So, tell us, Mr. Mantis,
what should we believe?

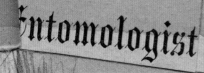

Praying mantises, also called mantids, hold
their front legs up together when resting, as
if they are praying. Look carefully: they appear
to be a part of the plant on which they rest.

19

Milkweed for Monarch

I'm very, very smart
and rather lucky,
I would say.

My diet is the milkweed plant.
I eat it every day.

Most usually, I'm hidden
when attackers choose to dine,
and birds don't like my milkweed taste.
How very, very fine!

This caterpillar is the larval stage of the monarch
butterfly. They eat only milkweed plants, which are
poisonous to birds. The milkweed leaves make the
caterpillars—and later the butterflies—poisonous, too.

Monarch and Friends

The monarch likes to travel
 in the company of others.
To Mexico,
 she drifts and glides—
  with moms and dads and brothers.

The butterfly life cycle has four stages: egg, larva, pupa, and adult. Monarch butterflies migrate to warm climates in the winter and return in the spring.

21

Termite Taste

Just imagine,
if you could,
a creepy crawler
crunching wood.

He fancies logs
and limbs, nutritious;
tree trunks, sweet
and quite delicious.

Could you,
would you,
find it great
to spy some sawdust
on your plate,
and hurry up to take a bite?
A very hungry termite might.

Termites are closely related to cockroaches.
Though they are best known for eating wood,
termites also like to eat cotton and paper.

Daddy, What Long Legs You Have!

This daddy has the longest legs.
What makes them even more so
is simply that he also has
a teeny, tiny torso.

raudoptera ... all kinds of insect b...
Riker specimen mounts at re...
and circulars free on apr...

...ccinellidæ of the world in exchange ; also biologica...
...hroclystia (Eupithecia) and Lithocolletis.—Dr Chr...
...swig, Germany.

...ccinellidæ of the world in exchange ; also biologica
...hroclystia (Eupithecia) and Lithocolletis.—Dr Chr
...swig, Germany.

Lepidoptera.

oh........213
........214
........218
Linn.......220
........221
........225
........238
........239
–II........242

Daddy longlegs is a long-legged creature often mistaken for a spider. Though they are arachnids, they have only two eyes, no fangs or venom, no silk spinnerets, and a single body instead of a body in two parts. Another name for daddy longlegs is harvestman. This arachnid has much in common with scorpions, mites, and ticks.

23

Grasshopper Green

Grasshopper Green is a munching machine,
he is built with precision and flair.

His hind legs are long and exceedingly strong,
like two springs as he zings through the air.

Four wings let him fly, let him zip through the sky,
he has jaws that are perfect for crunching.

With ears near his knees and five eyes, sure to please,
he spends most of his time simply munching.

Like all insects, a grasshopper has three main body sections: the head, the thorax, and the abdomen. They can leap many times their body length. When scared or stressed, they spit out a brown liquid, often known as tobacco juice.

INDIAN INSECTS.—1,000 species (200 named), (Lepidoptera and Odonata in papers); All of for Diptera of world (preferred); perfect condition General Post Office, Calcutta, India. or self cheap. E. BR HIPPODAMIA in numbers wanted for variation or moths, especially *H. maesta, 13-maculata, simulata* JOHNSON, Station for Experimental Evolution, Cold Spring COLEOPTERA.—Aleochariidae wanted

Spinning Spiny-Back

I spin,

and spin,

and when I need

a peppy picker-upper,

I spin a little more,

and then

I eat my web for supper.

Spiny-backs are orb weavers. When they build a new web, they take down the old one and eat the discarded silk, which is a great source of protein. Spiny-backs are champion recyclers.

Flies Fly

A hungry fly, with sticky feet,
decides he wants a bite to eat.
He scans the scene with giant eyes,
surveys the cakes and chocolate pies,
dips down and hovers, starts to rise,
and—like a helicopter—F L I E S *

Flies are insects with only two wings. They belong to the order Diptera, which comes from two Greek words: *di*, meaning "two," and *pteron*, meaning "wing." The buzzing of a fly is the sound of its beating wings.

27

Cockroach Love (Really?)

I am not loved, not loved at all.
I'm not like any other.
But surely someone cares for me.
I think it is my MOTHER.

Cockroaches have been on earth for 320 million years, existing even before the dinosaurs. They are very fast runners with strong and sturdy legs.

28

Mosquito Bites!

Oh no! It's Mosquito!
Oh drat. She is back.

She's ready and eager
to make an attack.

With family and friends,
she hangs out in a ditch.

Her probing proboscis
produces an itch

that comes from the bump
that will follow the bite,

with itching and scratching
from morning 'til night!

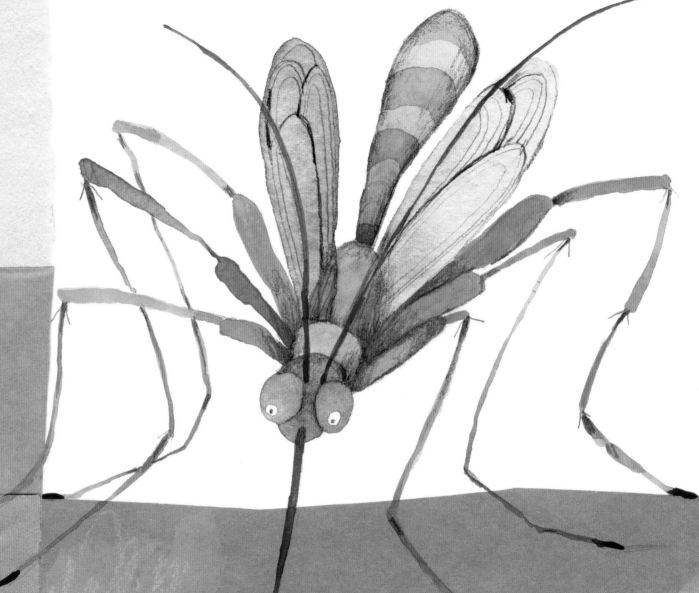

 Mosquito comes from *mosca*, the Spanish word for a fly. A mosquito's wings move up to a thousand times per second. One of the largest mosquitoes is the gallinipper, which can grow as big as a quarter.

29

Three Cheers for Jewelwing

I feast on mosquitoes.
I eat 'em, I do.
I feed on mosquitoes,
and *they* feed on you!

Ebony jewelwing is a damselfly, usually found near water. The young live below the surface of a pond or stream. Jewelwing eats massive numbers of insects, especially mosquitoes.

June Bug Whoosh

June bugs, July bugs,
and flip-flashing fly-bugs.
They're lured by the light,
all those high-in-the-sky bugs.

Whizzing and whirling
in fabulous flight.
Whooshing like rockets
to tell us "good night."

June bugs are nocturnal and like to swarm around streetlights, porch lights, and lights at ballparks. Females lay eggs in midsummer. The young spend winter underground as white grubs. They feed on the roots of trees and grasses and on crops like lettuce and strawberries.

Fruit Fly Fantasy

They seem to arise
from bananas and pears,

then capture the table
and circle the chairs.

Oh, where do they come from
and where do they go?

They stage an invasion
and vanish like snow.

Fruit flies seem to appear as if by magic. They grow to adulthood through a supershort, weeklong cycle of metamorphosis from eggs that have been deposited on the surface of fermenting foods.

Par-*tick*-u-lar-ly Awesome

No wonder that the tiny tick
seems so abundant, often thick.
The female lays (now here's the scoop)
five thousand eggs—in one fell swoop!

Ticks are parasites that feed on the blood of animals,
including people. Deer ticks are to be avoided because
they can carry Lyme disease. Choose a buddy and have a
tick inspection after walking in the woods or high grass.

33

Mite-y Nice Advice

Mites may dwell on musty shelves
and dine on moldy glue.

On pages of forgotten books,
no doubt you'll find a few.

But if you'll read this book each day,
we won't begin to chew.

We could invade! We haven't yet.
That's *our* advice to you.

Most mites are microscopic creatures, similar to ticks and spiders but much smaller. They feed on mold, bacteria, and even dead skin cells.

Be Mine, Honeybee

Don't worry, little honeybee.
No one will bother you.
Your sting's a part of nature,
sometimes you get frightened, too.

You're making wax for candle glow
and honey for our toast.
You power up the flowers,
and that's what we like the most.

Honeybees live in colonies made up of a queen, female workers, and
male drones. Honeybees are crucial in the pollination of fruits, vegetables,
and other crops. Just the females—including the queen—have stingers,
and they sting only when frightened. Enjoy watching but take care.

35

Firefly Finale

We glitter and glimmer
and put on a show
in honor of Earth—
come and share in our glow!

The twinkle of the firefly, or lightning bug, is a cold light,
produced without much heat. The glow comes from a chemical
reaction inside the body of this small, fascinating beetle. Be on
the lookout for fireflies at night—and share in the glow.

CRICKET NOTES

CRICKETS are related to katydids and grasshoppers. The female has a long spike at the end of her abdomen for laying eggs. Both katydids and crickets are favorite music makers because of their summer evening serenades.

ANTS live in highly organized colonies, with at least one queen, many female workers, and males for breeding. The common little black ant we see most often is native to North America. There are about ten thousand different species throughout the world.

CICADAS are large, clumsy bugs with a big sound. The males are equipped with a special ribbed membrane called a tymbal, which their strong muscles bend inward to make a vibrating click. An air chamber in their abdomen amplifies their song. In effect, they have their own sound system. There are more than 160 species of cicadas in North America.

JUMPING SPIDERS are generally small and can be quite colorful; there are more than five thousand varieties. Their jumping feats depend on the weight and posture of the spider and the silk it has spun.

DRAGONFLIES have been on earth for millions of years. Some scientists believe that early dragonflies were the largest insects, with wingspans of two and a half feet! Dragonflies are fast-food experts and munch their prey on the go. They are excellent fliers and look like shiny jewels dancing in the sky.

INCHWORM is a whimsical term given to the larvae of moths. Inchworms are similar to caterpillars but have small, hairless bodies and no middle legs, which makes them move with a looping gait. This has given rise to the idea that they are measuring each inch as they crawl.

LADYBUGS are also called ladybird beetles. Males and females look alike; the female, on close observation, is slightly larger. They are small bugs with a big appetite for crop-damaging aphids. Gardeners and farmers can buy ladybugs for aphid control.

BUMBLEBEES are native to North America and Great Britain. They are excellent pollinators and are often placed in nest boxes in greenhouses to pollinate hot-house tomatoes. Because they wear hairy coats, they are able to fly in cooler temperatures than honeybees.

DUNG BEETLES like decaying vegetables and chicken feathers as well as fungus and mold. Dung beetles are also called scarab beetles, even though the scarab beetle family includes dung beetles, June bugs, rhinoceros beetles, Japanese beetles, and more. The females of some species lay their eggs in balls of dung that are rolled up by the males. The female carefully grooms the dung ball until her babies emerge from the eggs.

SPOTTED WATER BEETLE is one of many beetles that likes lakes and ponds—even swimming pools. They are large bugs, capable of diving as well as swimming. They propel themselves by using their hind legs as oars.

ROLY-POLY BUGS are well known by those who enjoy being outdoors. They can be found around yards and houses and are important decomposers of rotting wood. They will roll up into a ball when threatened. When danger passes, they will stretch out and crawl back to their nests.

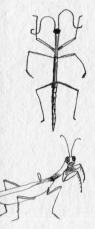

WALKING STICKS are amazing creatures. They are disguised as sticks or stems and move slowly. Two common varieties are the northern walking stick and the giant walking stick. Some walking sticks can regrow a lost limb.

PRAYING MANTIS is an odd-looking insect because of the way it holds itself. There are many different species, including the European, the Chinese, and the Carolina. About twenty different species reside in North America. They vary in color, but all have a folded front leg position, as if they are holding their hands in prayer.

MONARCH BUTTERFLY is the most famous butterfly and is easily recognized by its orange and black colors. This beauty migrates to California and Mexico for the winter. Monarch is a brush-footed butterfly: its small front legs are covered with bristles. The monarch caterpillar is brightly striped yellow, black, and white and feeds on the milkweed plant.

TERMITES are famous for eating wood. Though they often damage homes and buildings, they help to clean up the earth by breaking down decaying matter. They are sometimes considered winged ants, but they are not ants because their wing and body construction is different. They live in colonies with a king, a queen, workers, and soldiers.

DADDY LONGLEGS is the more common name for a harvestman. Surprisingly, some daddy longlegs have short legs. Males have smaller bodies but longer legs than females. These creatures hold their bodies close to the ground. If one is caught by its leg, the leg may break away from the body and grow back again. There are about 225 species in North America and 4,500 to 5,000 in the world.

GRASSHOPPERS come in many colors, which are their camouflage. Some are spotted; some are striped to look like blades of grass. There is even a rainbow grasshopper. Grasshoppers can be quite destructive, wiping out farm crops and other vegetation in a very short time.

SPINY-BACK SPIDER is one of many types of orb weavers. Female spiny-backs have spines that jut out of her hard abdomen. Orb weavers have poor vision and discover their victims by feeling vibrations in their webs. After their victims get caught in the web, the spiders wrap them up like mummies in the silk they spin. Orb weavers are found all over the world.

FLIES have a big presence on our planet. The housefly is the most commonly known member of the family, but there are many types of flies in our world. Some of the more interesting (or annoying) types include the horsefly, the flower fly, greenheads, stilt-legged flies with skinny legs, and thick-headed flies with thick heads.

COCKROACHES have a bad reputation. They are accused of being the result of poor housekeeping. Actually, cockroaches, like dragonflies, existed before both dinosaurs and houses. The hissing cockroach in Madagascar is especially startling. It hisses by forcing air out of breathing holes underneath its body. Some female cockroaches make excellent mothers. They carry their eggs inside their abdomen to keep them from harm.

MOSQUITOES are abundant in summertime, especially after periods of rain. Their eggs are laid on the surface of water and soon hatch into larvae (wrigglers), which grow into pupae (tumblers). The females feast on blood, which provides protein to produce yet more mosquitoes. In addition to people and other mammals, mosquitoes bite birds and amphibians. Mosquitoes can spread dangerous diseases like malaria and the Zika virus.

JEWELWING is a damselfly. Though most damselflies live near streams and rivers, ebony jewelwing also ventures into forests. The male is a beautiful, shiny blue green. The female is lighter and softer in color. Damselflies are closely related to dragonflies.

JUNE BUG is the better-known name for the light-loving insects also called May beetles. They are abundant on early summer evenings, flying wildly toward porch lights and window screens, making lots of noise and crashing here and there. There are many variations in both color and size. Adults feed on plants and grasses.

FRUIT FLIES, also called pomace flies, are often seen hovering around fruit on a countertop or table. Though bothersome, they are important in genetic research because the larvae possess unusually large chromosomes in their salivary glands, which scientists can easily see with a microscope.

TICKS and **MITES** are closely related. They reside in many places but are mostly unseen because they are so small. Many mites are microscopic parasites that feed on plants and animals. More than 30,000 species have been named, and there are undoubtedly more. Ticks are larger parasites that feed on other animals, including humans.

HONEYBEES are a crucial link in the food chain; they were introduced to North America in 1622 by colonists in Jamestown, Virginia. They are experts at pollination and are essential for growing crops, flowers, and other vegetation. These small bees are very social insects. They live in colonies consisting of one queen, thousands of female workers, and several hundred male drones. Honeybees are experiencing hard times and are declining in number. Their plight is being carefully studied in hopes that the problem will soon be solved.

FIREFLIES are small beetles. They are also known as lightning bugs. Fireflies send one another various signals with different flash patterns. The color can also vary, from yellow to green. Fireflies are one of our most appealing insects. Watching and counting flashes can be a great way to spend a summer evening.